A RECOLLECTION OF LOVE, LOSS, AND THOUGHTS
THAT WERE NOT NEARLY AS DEEP AS I THOUGHT

a recollection of love,
loss, and thoughts that
were not nearly as deep
as i thought

amber christine walton

Charleston, SC
www.PalmettoPublishing.com

A Recollection of Love, Loss, and Thoughts That Were Not Nearly as Deep as I Thought
Copyright © 2020 by Amber Christine Walton

ISBN-13: 978-1-64990-028-9
ISBN-10: 1-64990-028-7

For Olivia,

Who has been my four-legged soulmate from the day we met, whose soft heartbeat spoke to me even in the darkest of nights, and whose soft pitter patter I refused to abandon by leaving this world. Thank you. I love you.

i hope that one day
i'll be able to
spill my thoughts
across thousands
and thousands
of pages
for the world to see
a recollection of
love
loss
and thoughts
that were not nearly
as deep
as i thought

you say that you want to read my poems

that you can appreciate all styles

of art

but my poems

are my release

they cannot be enjoyed

with a cup of tea

in front of a fire ablaze

but they can be felt

like the suffering that wrote them

in due time

we will see

if you truly can appreciate

the sweet anguish

that dances

a fire ablaze

amongst these pages

life may tell you

to grab poetic moments

run to your journal

and capture every one of them

but i whisper

ever so softly

in life's ear

all moments are poetic

i'm not sure
why the term
lone wolf
is so popular
why it is sometimes
admired
for wolves
are pack animals
constantly building each other up
embodying
strength in numbers
i know the lone wolf
it lingers in disappointment
failure
sadness
loneliness
because wolves
are meant to be
together

i absolutely dread
this mysterious
aching
anguish
i feel so weighted down
as if walking alone
could make me
a champion powerlifter
but anyone
who has lifted weights
knows
nothing is as heavy
as grief in your bones
emptiness in your soul
and the lack
of a sense of belonging
the weight
is insufferable

the sadness i feel
has this romantic way
of making loneliness
feel like the only lover i'll ever need
like a drug
it intoxicates me
and rocks me
into a numb state of existence
where i will eventually perish
because i keep coming back
to the one stable thing i have
the constant state
of being
alone

when i was a child
my mother gave me
a book
because i was a sad little girl
the book was blue
it was called
the blue day book
it was supposed to make you feel
less alone
when i was in school
the kids called me
a name
because i was a sad little girl
the name was "blue"
it was supposed to make you feel
like it wouldn't last
i'm an adult now
my doctor gave me a pill
because i'm still
just a sad little girl
the pills are blue
they've been called
a last resort
they're supposed to make you feel
happy
they don't

is there anything to be said
for grief
when you are fighting
an uphill battle
but you are still
fighting

i'm not sure
if i'm good
at anything
aside from
being sad

a gentle
pitter-patter
a soft
heartbeat
at my feet
it's comforting to know
that someone knows
i'm not okay

you say you wrote the girl a poem
the one who lends a smile to the world
when she doesn't even have one to spare
you say you have a rough draft
for the drifter exploring dimensions
ever so slowly
but it could never be rough enough
to encompass the pain that grazes
across her skin
like sandpaper
and the emptiness that dances
where her soul should find its home

there is an inexpressible
amount of pain
in loss
not in a day
not in a week
not in a year
the pain lasts
much longer
than our stipend
of grief
the pain lasts
forever
but beyond the depths
of grief
my soul has found asylum
in a begrudging coexistence
amongst the pain

loneliness

is not just a sensation

it's otherworldly

it's unexplainable

it's suffocating

i can feel my soul

attempting to escape

this hollow shell

in effort to find

someone

somewhere

something

because even in a crowded room

i am still

incredibly

lonely

yet again
i bring myself back
to the lingering question:
who would love a girl
whose poems
don't even rhyme
imperfection
her fatal flaw
so here i sit
an orphan of these pages
with my unrhymed
unrythymed
unloved
soul

it's 3am
i am awake
and in love
i have never
been so content
with lying awake
at 3am
in all my life

i feel as though my soul
spent lifetimes
searching for yours
scanning every busy street
and every empty room
in every dimension
of my monochrome world
until we locked eyes
you took my breath away
and i'm still searching for the words
to explain the color
that you have brought into my world
my poems
are so full of you
and my soul
is finally
at ease

you think i'm silly
crazy if you will
for liking the movies
and the books
full of dystopia
and believing
the world will follow
in close pursuit
i'm okay with dying
in a perfect world
the crazy old woman
who buried her coins in tin cans
and never trusted the world around her
and believed
in those old movies
and books
a little too much
i hope you know
that i love you
and i hope that when you tell them
about the crazy old woman
who liked the crazy old movies
and books
a little too much
that you'll tell them
it was nurture
not nature
it's always nurture

i just don't understand
what happens
when we die
i just can't accept
that our soulless bodies
turn cold
and that's it
because my body
is as cold as the winter
yet here i am

i know
that people think
that my poetry
is not real poetry
it's unrythymed
and unrhymed
to me
it's real
and raw
as i would speak
choked up
and unsure
those who believe
that my poems
are not poems
are infatuated
with color
in a world
they cannot see

i want to write my vows
because the only two things
that i've gotten right
in my short time on this earth
have been my writing
and you
i believe that to read off a
scripted
overused
outdated
set of words
that are not my own
is rather unromantic
for a writer
i want to show everyone
from my own tongue
that although there may only be
two things that i've gotten right
in my short time on this earth
those things are
my writing
and you
and that's more than i thought
i would ever have

i think very few people
truly understand
the unequivocal tranquility
in the sunrise
and i think
that may be what's wrong
with the world

you once gave me
a book called
being forgetful
but
even when i try
i really
can't seem
to remember
how it went

i would like to believe
faith in humanity
isn't synonymous with
being naïve
i don't refuse to see
the empty side of the glass
i seldom pay attention
to the volume
of what occupies the glass
i choose to believe
that no matter
where the liquid may lie
it is always able
to be replenished

i had too much baggage
to carry myself
so you offered to help
which was so kind
i just hope
that i haven't given you
concrete shoes
in this sea of loneliness
or worse-
suffocated you
above the water
with my unwillingness
to lose you

i think i took up gardening
because in a world
where everything is
broken
and crumbling
i can take something
that is practically nothing
and help it grow
with just a bit of
love
and care
but i'm not sure
that i could ever plant enough
life
to drown out the despair
these days

i saw you read my poems
but i like to pretend
that you haven't
because there is no other feeling
quite like unleashing your feelings
in an unraveled mess
only to be greeted with
the chilling reality
of silence

my poems are forged
atop the slowly smoldering coals
of loneliness
and sorrow
i feel as if
i would be lost without
the loneliness
and sorrow
because eventually
the soul finds comfort
in desolation

i dream of my poetry
reaching out
touching souls
but i have nightmares of my poetry
being read
stealing joy
and crushing everything in its path
i'm not sure
if that is just
the looming shadow
of fear

i always become nervous
as i sit in a waiting room
and i have no concept of time
but what is time
other than some
meaningless concept
created to put limitations
on the forever
i want to spend with you

i've drifted through existence
afraid
of the sadness
afraid
of what it was doing
to my relationships
to my mind
to my future
afraid
to tell a single soul
afraid
of the medication
afraid
of my acceptance
yet i'm still so
afraid
to lose it

the other day
you said
that i was the physical embodiment
of everything a writer is:
morose
sentimental
lonely
and i think
we as writers are all so similar
because we are all so infatuated with the idea
of a romantic and selfless society
that when we start
to write
about the romantic and selfless societies
we realize
how dark and sinister humanity really is
and we realize
that the dark and sinister humanity
is inescapable
so we grow into
grouchy
depressed
cynical people
until we can isolate ourselves
into our blissful ignorance
where everything is good
once again

sometimes i feel clingy
and i think you feel it too
but i don't think you understand
that every lifetime before this one
i have eventually lost you
to the abrupt awakening
of mortality
and i don't think you understand
that this time
my soul has been
wading through the loneliness
searching high and low
yearning for yours
for twenty one years
this time around
i refuse to lose you
like i have
every lifetime before this one
to the abrupt awakening
of mortality
please don't leave my soul
wading
searching
yearning
for another twenty one years

i have stopped writing
for the last few months
i have lost my muse
and the scariest thing is
i don't feel
the urge
for it to return

when i finally decide
that it is time
to give myself an eternal rest
don't believe
the believers
who say it was an act of sin
for there is no greater sin
than their god's sin
of watching
his people
live in misery

instead
tell them
to believe
that i died
of a broken heart
that was no sin of mine

innocence
is a beautiful thing
you robbed me
of my innocence
and distract me
by calling me
a child

i love neon signs
they transport me back to a time
when i was blissfully
walking down a street
at 2am
and i realized
it wasn't so blissful
and i was as sad as the neon signs
illuminating the night
at 2am
for no one to see
their bright urgent cries
ringing through the air
desperate to be
seen
heard
loved
just as i was
at 2am
so now i look at the neon signs
and the feeling is beautifully
and hopelessly
romantic
the esoteric loneliness

they say
that the eyes are windows
to the soul
but i do not agree
because they also say
that my eyes are beautiful
yet fail to realize
my soul
pounding on the windows
and begging for release

i long for a sense
of belonging
and an end
to this loneliness
just as you long for me
to be present
in this moment

i smell
the smoke
and i see
the beautiful embers
of my soul
burning to the ground
still i feel
nothing

they say poetry
in the moment
we occupy
has become so
dry
superficial
unrhythymed
they say poetry
in the moment
we occupy
could not be
real poetry
maybe i am
dry
superficial
unrythymed
maybe i am not
a real poet
but when did it become
so wrong
to just write

sometimes i become
so numb
that i feel
i have slowly faded
out of existence
then you come back
and make me feel
the soul crushing reality
of inadequacy
and i realize
once again
i am still doomed to this state
of existence

if i had
the words
to express the way
my soul aches
the words
may just kill me
and that would be okay

when it is late
at night
and the world
is hushed
i lay back
and the trauma
seeps in
to surround me
and carry me off
into a never-ending world
of pain
and the realization
that you may have never
actually
loved me

i wonder
if there is anyone out there
as broken
and shattered
as i am
if you're reading this
i am here
in these words
with you

do you ever look up at the stars
and hear them whisper
all of the little things
you were meant to do
how you were meant to achieve
greatness
and there you sit
unable to roam the overwhelming world
unable to function even with the assistance
of the medication
because i do
every day
i disappoint the stars
every day

i always wished
that i could fly
that i could leave my body
just for a moment
to float
then came the dissociation
now i sit
begging the universe
for a grip on reality
please –

if your reading this
and my poetry has finally reached you
i hope my mind
has hushed
and my bones
have rested
peacefully
six feet under

i want

more than anything

to share

my poetry

but it would shock

the world

and disappoint

everyone

sometimes i feel
completely invisible
that if i screamed
not a soul would hear
that if i reached out
not a soul would see
do you think
that it's because
when i should have spoken up
i didn't

i have been broken
so terribly
that i have crumbled
into a fine dusting
just waiting
for the wind
to carry me away

i can remember
the last time
i was absolutely
shattered
your tongue
was so sharp
blood started to drip
from my nose
down my face
forming a puddle
on my bathroom counter
it was then
that i realized
you were destroying me
from the inside-out

you are so pure
i can see it
through your eyes
as they whisper the tales
of a thousand
beautiful
wonders
ever so softly
in the night
when i look
into your eyes
just for a moment
i feel the darkness
slowly losing
its breathtaking grasp
it has upon me
i would endure
a thousand
torturous days
to preserve the purity
of your soul
and to keep feeling
those moments
forever

is my soul
beautifully damaged
or did i
just damage
what was once
beautiful

oh
i apologize
please don't allow
my trauma
to ruin your evening

how can you wave
your empty
suicide threats
so liberally
in my face
when you know
the thought
is so active
in my mind

it's difficult
trying to fit
into a loving family
where you'll never belong
after all these years
because all your life
you've been taught
that everyone lies
everyone leaves
and everyone likes to watch you bleed
it's difficult
trying to fit
into a loving family
because after all these years
the thought
of your past
is always looming

i have not written
any poems
in awhile
my thoughts
are so
sporadic
all i can do
is float
atop the sea
of fear
loneliness
and rejection
but sometimes
i wallow
and i hope
i do not

i feel so
detached
from reality
as if
i am a
little
astronaut
floating
in the
engulfing
darkness

i just need
to rest my bones
for a very
very
very
long time

i try
to drown out
the thoughts
that break me down
through the core
of my being
but i know
the only way
to succeed
would be to
slip
away
softly
into an endless
eternity
as my lungs
slowly fill

sometimes i think
i need to surrender myself
to the clutches
of a sanatorium
but i worry
because isn't feeling trapped
why i'm here

of the few things i still remember
of my elementary school days
i remember the thought
of freezing
to death
seemed so peaceful
in all of the books they seemed to
just drift
into an everlasting rest
i remember wanting that
so badly
as i searched for the bus
with my barbie backpack
that seemed to engulf me
please
engulf me

at the end
of the day
there is
nothing
left
and i'm not sure
if anyone
anywhere
could ever
come back
from nothing

the darkness
always seems to creep
through my eager mind
to settle
in the depths
of my cavernous
heart

it's like
i crave death
so badly
but everything
is fine

the blood runs
so slowly
through my veins
my body went cold
long before
i took my last breath

if you're reading this
after my untimely demise
don't feel bad
for i had
an inebriating romance
with the sadness
and the numbness
that being sober
brought me

the voices in my head
are especially loud today
i need silence
but the silence
amplifies the voices

this sadness

is not

a raincloud that follows me

for clouds

they are weightless

but this sadness

is a thousand chains

this sadness

is unbearably heavy

the masks
make me feel
more detached
than the people
behind them

you left

and now

i feel my grasp

on reality

on you

slipping away

slowly

i live in a world

apart from the rest

i see my demons

and hear my enemies

my life a mirage

and yet

i still

don't see

you

i just feel
so drained
there's nowhere
to express it
but these pages
i'm not sure
how i feel
that no one
will
ever
read them